Why Read the Bible?

Sharon Daugherty

Why Read the Bible?
Copyright © 2024 Sharon Daugherty
Sharon Daugherty
Victory Christian Center Inc.
Tulsa, Oklahoma 74136-7700 USA
www.Victory.com

ISBN # 978-1-964492-03-2.

Table of Contents

Introduction

My First Spiritual Encounter Marked My Life

I got saved, as well as my late husband, during the Jesus Revolution days. The Holy Spirit hit our little town of Magnolia, Arkansas, in the spring of 1970. Kids were getting radically saved and becoming spiritually hungry for the Word of God and for all that the Holy Spirit was doing. We wanted to fellowship together and seek God. The hippie drug culture had just started in the US. It was Satan's attempt to distract the young generation away from God. We were beginning to hear about the outdoor wild youth concerts like Woodstock and the riots elsewhere. But God moved in our town, and God moved in various cities across the US.

I've been reminded of this again as Wilmore, Kentucky, experienced another outpouring of the Holy Spirit in March 2023 like it did in 1970. The Holy Spirit was moving all over the US in various places. I believe there were people who prayed for this back then and have prayed for this right now.

Understand this: Satan will not win! We have heard prophetic words over and over in these past decades of this last great move of God that will hit the present generation and multitudes will be brought into the kingdom of God because of this last day harvest.

Right after I was radically saved, I wanted to read the Bible. Before that time, I had thought it was boring. When my mom saw I was interested, she bought a *Living Bible New Testament* called *The Way* for me. It had just come out. It was a paperback book and had pictures throughout the pages of teenagers that looked like kids I knew. It was easy to read because it was in our present-day language. I prayed, "Lord, make it interesting to me for seven days in a row, and I'll read it the rest of my life." He did, and I did!

Just like there is no one who was born a baby who has remained a baby, spiritually speaking we are born as spiritual babies, and we are destined to grow. (See 1 John 2:12–14.)

We grow from baby to child to teen to young adult to older adult. We grow by feeding on the Word, exercising and doing what we learn along the way.

First Peter 2:2 GW says, "Desire God's pure word as newborn babies desire milk. Then you will grow in your salvation."

Growth doesn't happen overnight. It is staying consistent over the years in what you learn to do. Growth takes time. Growth will be evident to other people.

I find it interesting that 1 Peter 2:2 starts with the word *desire*. *Desire* is "to long for or have an impulse for something that you know will be beneficial and bring satisfaction." When we read or study God's Word, it brings a sense of satisfaction that something supernatural is working in our lives. We may not understand it all, but we can sense something changing us. That's because God's Word has the anointing of the Holy Spirit, and His Spirit is working in us as we read or study it.

Chapter 1

Learning God's Voice

Jesus said, "My sheep hear my voice, and I know them, and they follow Me" (John 10:27).

When I surrendered my life to Jesus Christ in April of 1970, I heard the voice of the Lord that night very strongly in my spirit. It was as if it was an audible voice speaking to me in my heart. He said three things:

1. Tonight I'm settling your salvation, and you will never doubt your salvation again. (I had questioned that in my heart knowing I had not fully surrendered my life to the Lord, at this point, so this was a needed word to my heart.)

2. I've called you into the ministry. (I had been thinking I would someday go to either New York or Hollywood because of my singing ability and stage performance growing up. That night those desires changed.)

3. Read your Bible and pray daily.

That week someone told me the following Scripture: "This is the record that God hath given to us eternal life and this life is in His Son" (1 John 5:11). I heard that little voice inside me confirm that the Scriptures were the record that I had received eternal life. I would no longer question my salvation after that.

I began reading that record—the Bible—daily. It seemed that God knew my thoughts and feelings as I read, and He answered those thoughts. I remember my brother telling me to underline in my Bible when a verse seemed to speak to me at a particular time of need and mark the date. As I did that this one day, I thought that God might feel offended that I didn't value all of the Bible since I had not underlined it all; so I went back and underlined my entire Bible. That probably sounds funny, but my relationship with the Lord was very simple and genuine.

When someone reads the Bible, they learn how God thinks and they learn His ways. Isaiah 55:8–9 says, "For my thoughts are not your thoughts, neither are your ways my ways, saith the Lord. For as the heavens are higher than the earth, so are my ways higher than your ways, and my thoughts than your thoughts."

"Higher" doesn't mean His thoughts and His ways are out of reach or impossible to know. It means His thoughts and His ways are better than our thoughts and our ways. Years ago there was a TV ad that said, "Ford has a better idea." As you read and study God's Word, you'll begin to see that, "God has a better idea."

Let God's Word Correct You

Early in my Christian walk, I had a tendency to compare myself with others. One day I picked up the Word of God and it fell open to 2 Corinthians 10:12. My paraphrase version of that verse says, "We are not to compare ourselves with others as some do, who measure themselves by themselves. These are not wise." I immediately realized God was giving me both a correction and an encouragement.

When we read the Word of God, the Word reads us. It's like looking into a mirror. When you look into a mirror, you then make adjustments to your hair or your face. When you look into God's Word, you'll want to make adjustments in your life (James 1:22–25). God wants us to have a simple heart-to-heart relationship with Him. He speaks to us in our heart, and He speaks to us when we read His Word. This is important to understand because you will face various situations, and you will hear various deceptive voices speaking into your thoughts; God's Word enables us to discern what is right and what is wrong.

You Can See Jesus

There is an old chorus, "Turn Your Eyes Upon Jesus." One day I thought, how do I turn my eyes upon Jesus if I can't see Him physically here?

I knew I could use my imagination as I worshiped Him to see Him in my mind. However, when I heard that Jesus and His Word are one, I realized every time I look at Scripture I'm turning my eyes on Jesus. "In the beginning the Word already existed. The Word was with God, and the Word was God" (John1:1 NLT).

When we don't want to read the Bible or know what it says, it is like saying we don't want to see Jesus or know Him more intimately, and we don't want to listen to what He says.

It is a daily choice and can become a daily habit. Your time in the Word keeps you spiritually healthy.

Chapter 2

How I Learned
to Discipline Myself

When I first started reading the Bible, I read the New Testament, Psalms and Proverbs because I understood these Scriptures. I had thought the Old Testament was harder to understand and that I might stop reading when I had to read all the names of people in Numbers and 1 Chronicles. After two years reading just the New Testament, Psalms, and Proverbs, I decided to venture into the Old Testament. I pressed through the parts I didn't understand or that I didn't think were speaking to me at the time. Praise God! I stayed with it!

It was later, when I attended Christ for the Nations Bible Institute in Dallas, Texas, that I heard the founder, Freida Lindsey, say that she read through her entire Bible every year. She encouraged us, as students, to read through our Bible every year because reading the Old Testament would help us understand the New Testament and how it all fits together. I began to do this each year—not to tell other people that I had done this but because I knew I needed it.

I remember one time a man came to me and said that his wife had read through her Bible seven times, as if she was an authority. I said to him "good." I didn't say anything else. However, I thought, sometimes people read through the Bible as an accomplishment to impress others. God looks at the motive of our heart.

When my late husband and I were youth pastors in the beginning of our marriage, he felt to have a discipleship group with about 12 teens. We used a Bible study plan which taught us the importance of Scripture memory. Later we heard the message of faith and Scripture confession. We put Scriptures by our bathroom mirror so we would say them each day. This helped us in our thinking, and I believe God used it to change us and to increase our faith.

About two years later, my husband created a packet with Scripture cards that had a Scripture on one side and a confession of the Scripture on the other side. This packet could fit easily and neatly in pocket or in a purse so a person could take it with them and speak Scripture over their life any time of the day. That year we gave thousands to graduates of three different schools: ORU, CFNI, RHEMA. It was seed we sowed because of how those schools had blessed our lives with the Word of God.

Discipline Is Wisdom Not Legalism

I remember hearing about a minister who said that you don't need to read your Bible daily because that is legalism and bondage. He said that God doesn't want you to feel you're in a legalistic relationship with Him. Listen to me. Disciplining yourself in God's Word daily is not legalism. It is sharpening your weapon against your enemy, Satan. If Jesus memorized the Word of God (the Torah) as a young Jewish boy and used it to speak against the enemy in His life, how much more do you and I need to put the Word of God in our lives and use it against our enemy! Some say, "Well, you can't take Scripture out of context and use it." My response to that is "Well, Jesus did."

1 Then Jesus was led by the Spirit into the wilderness to be tempted there by the devil.
2 For forty days and forty nights he fasted and became very hungry.
3 During that time the devil came and said to him, "If you are the Son of God, tell these stones to become loaves of bread."
4 But Jesus told him, "No! The Scriptures say, People do not live by bread alone, but by every word that comes from the mouth of God."
5 Then the devil took him to the holy city, Jerusalem, to the highest point of the Temple,
6 and said, "If you are the Son of God, jump off! For the Scriptures say, 'He will order his angels to protect you. And they will hold you

up with their hands so you won't even hurt you foot on stone.'"

7 Jesus responded, "The Scriptures also say, 'You must not test the Lord your God.'"

8 Next the devil took him to the peak of a very high mountain and showed him all the kingdoms of the world and their glory.

9 "I will give it all to you," he said, "if you will kneel down and worship me."

10 "Get out of here, Satan," Jesus told him, "For the Scriptures say, 'You must worship the Lord your God and serve only him.'"

11 Then the devil went away, and angels came and took care of Jesus. (Matthew 4:1–11 NLT)

Jesus spoke "It is written" three times when the devil came to tempt Him, and the devil finally left Him for a season.

Having a disciplined time reading your Bible is not for show. When you do something out of the discipline of the Holy Spirit, you are doing it because you know that discipline will do you good in the long run. Any athlete understands this principle. Athletes know they have to practice daily to get better at their sport.

Another thought is that God's Word washes us on the inside as we read it. A person could say that you don't have to take a shower daily or brush your teeth daily because that's legalism. However, people you encounter during the day will appreciate that you have showered and brushed your teeth. People experience your life whether or not you've spent some time with God and are seeking to learn His thoughts and His ways. They can tell the difference. People can tell if you've spent time with the Lord. It comes out in your attitude and the way you respond to people in conversation.

Years ago, my late husband and I were on a ministry trip. I overslept one morning, and my husband had left the room to go walk and pray on the grounds where we were staying. When he returned, we were having a conversation and he asked me, " Have you had your time with the Lord this morning?"

I responded with somewhat of an irritation, "Not yet, but I was about to."

He then said, "I can tell." I knew he was right.

We had a good relationship where we spoke openly with each other. We had decided not to take offense when we felt corrected. I will admit it did still sting somewhat.

It hit me. I realized how very evident it is to others when we don't spend time putting God's Word in our lives and having a prayer time. Our attitude reflects this. God loves us, but He wants us to continue growing in Him. Today I still realize I need to allow God to keep working on me all my life. (See 2 Timothy 3:14–17.)

Some people like to pick and choose Scripture and reject whatever they don't like. That's like eating only sweets and not eating the foods that your body needs for fuel. I've learned not to pick and choose Scripture but to take the whole counsel of God's Word and let it speak to me. It all makes sense if you stay with it. It's all connected.

There are certain Scriptures that I speak regularly over my life because I know I depend upon those truths. For example, I have a list of Scriptures that I now have memorized over the years that apply to who I am in Christ, my authority over the devil, healing, freedom, provision, protection, peace of mind, guidance, and victory. These Scriptures now come out of me naturally when I pray. As we put Scripture in our memory bank, it becomes our weapon against the enemy's negative thoughts.

Chapter 3

Why Spiritual Disciplines?

A few years ago there was a teaching in the body of Christ that became very popular, but it was off balance. It sounded good, but several of those teaching it removed moral boundaries to the point that it didn't matter how a person lived saying that grace would cover it all. Many who had been continuing their spiritual disciplines of daily time in the Word and time in prayer recognized the error. Other people who felt they didn't need to discipline themselves in keeping time with the Lord believed the error. They believed that those who were disciplining themselves in taking time in God's Word were legalistic.

There are always those who simply follow the latest teacher who sounds good. But a tree is known by its fruit. Look at the fruit of a teaching you have heard. The Holy Spirit and the Word will always agree. Paul warned us about this:

> 3 For the time is coming when people will no
> longer listen to sound and wholesome teaching.

> They will follow their own desires and will look for teachers who will tell them whatever their itching ears want to hear.
>
> 4 They will reject the truth and chase after myths.
>
> 5 But you should keep a clear mind in every situation. (2 Timothy 4:3–5 NLT)

We witnessed a friend of ours who had been saved during the Jesus Movement of the 1970s, the same time that we had, lose his commitment that he made to the Lord. He made bad decisions and ended up with heartache and trouble that could have been avoided. We found out later that he had not established a disciplined time in the Bible or a prayer relationship with the Lord. He dropped out of church, as well, and went back to his old friends who pulled him back in a wrong direction.

Continuing in the truth of God's established Word is so important. Always look at the fruit of people. Compare what you see with those who tend to jump on any new fad they hear.

> 6 Just as you accepted Christ Jesus as your Lord, you must continue to follow Him.
>
> 7 Let your roots grow down into him, and let your lives be built on him. Then your faith will grow strong in the truth you were taught, and you will overflow with thankfulness.
>
> 8 Don't let anyone capture you with empty philosophies and high-sounding nonsense that come from human thinking and from

the spiritual powers of this world, rather than from Christ. (Colossians 2:6–8 NLT)

When we are putting God's Word in our hearts regularly, that Word will be in there for the Holy Spirit to draw upon when we are evaluating what we hear.

There's been a push by some to embrace a mindset labeled "woke ideology." It is not anything new. It's been around a long time. In fact, it's based on rebellion against God, which is what the serpent did in tempting Eve and Adam in the Garden of Eden so he could interfere with their relationship with God and take their authority. There was a man, Karl Marx, who many say made the woke theory known. The teaching is to remove a God-consciousness and bring a revolution in a country so its government can be overthrown and taken over by a small group. Marx was an atheist and his ideology is *atheism*. It does not offer hope for change in a person and does not encourage a person to believe in God.

There are professors in schools and universities who teach that there is no absolute truth and that the Bible contradicts itself, so you can't believe the Bible. They try to make man to be his own god, but there comes a point where man's understanding is limited. We are taught to exalt the Lord, who is unlimited.

The devil wants to overthrow God's authority in your life, and he wants to take over your life to destroy you. This is why you must be smarter than the devil. This is why you need to know the truth of God's Word. This is why you need to maintain your spiritual disciplines.

Chapter 4

Avoid Deception

I remember hearing that years ago if a bank was going to hire a bank teller, they would have the person handle genuine paper money and then slip them a counterfeit bill to see if they detected it as they were counting. If they detected the counterfeit, they were hired. If they didn't, they were not hired.

People can ultimately recognize the difference in someone who is genuine in their faith and someone who knows how to perform being nice so that they will look good to others.

The more we handle God's Word in life the more we will detect what is false and what is true. We will become more discerning about counterfeit and deceptive people and situations. The more we put God's Word in our lives, the more we will discern in ourselves our attitudes and any deceptive thoughts or words. We will more readily recognize deceptive teaching of others or deceptive circumstances we might find ourselves in. We will be more discerning about people we come in contact with in order to speak His words into their lives.

I have seen believers become deceived just as Eve was deceived by the cunning ways of the serpent in the Garden like Paul warned in 2 Corinthians 11:3–4. Sincere Christians can become deceived. Satan watches for people who do not know Scripture well, or are living in sin and have become vulnerable, gullible, and tolerant of anyone who comes their way. Sometimes people are deceived by a personality they like on TV or someone they meet who sounds good but has a slightly different bent on a message which is deceptive. Discernment doesn't have to be spooky. It should be very normal in our lives.

Years ago a woman came to me and said her husband had left her for another woman. He and the other woman were attending another church in our city. His wife asked him if he and the woman did not feel convicted of their sin of adultery when they were in church. He told her, "My reality is not the same as your reality. No, we don't feel convicted."

I prayed with her that the Holy Spirit would go after him and convict him of sin and draw him back to his wife. A few months later he contacted her and asked if he could come back and reestablish his marriage relationship with her. She was willing to forgive and get counsel. He returned, and they received counsel together. God saved their marriage. However, he became swallowed up in guilt and depression over his sin. He couldn't forgive himself.

He gave into the negative thoughts of the devil and took his life.

We are living in the end times, and Jesus said seducing, deceiving spirits would pull people to leave their faith and believe negative thoughts. (See 1 John 4:1.) Recognizing the spiritual battle we are in, we must become discerning.

Second Timothy 3:13 NKJV says, "Evil men and imposters will grow worse and worse, deceiving and being deceived." We've watched how this world's woke culture has tried to invade the minds and hearts of some believers to quit viewing the Bible as relevant for today. There was a popular worship leader who announced he was going through "deconstruction" of everything he had been taught to believe from the Bible. He didn't realize that the spirits in this world were actually deceiving him.

Here is the key to avoiding deception:

- Continue in God's Word! Make it final authority in your life.

- Evaluate everything around you by the Word of God. It's the highest truth, and it can help you discern what people are saying around you and what the world is saying to try to squeeze you into its mold.

- Stay connected with church and with other believers who are seeking to grow in their relationship with God, with His Word and prayer.

We have to choose to make God's Word final authority in our lives; and when we do, we will see the results of it.

The Word Discerns Between Soul and Spirit

Hebrews 4:12 NKJV says, "The word of God is living and powerful, and sharper than any two-edged sword, piercing even to the division of soul and spirit, and of joints and marrow, and is a discerner of the thoughts and intents of the heart."

I remember my daughters had two friends growing up who were twins. The twins looked exactly alike, in my opinion. I could not tell them apart. I asked my daughters how they could differentiate between the two girls. They said, "Mom, it's easy. One has a very tiny mole on her cheek and the other doesn't. One has a more pronounced personality and the other one is shy."

I said. "I don't have time to look that closely when I'm just saying hello." My daughters had been spending time with the two girls, so they immediately knew them apart when they would see them. That reminded me of the fact that when we spend time with the Word of God, we will more easily see whatever is false when it comes around.

God's Word discerns us as we read it. His Word discerns our thoughts and motives. In order to discern, God's Word separates what is of our soul (our feelings, our mental reasonings, and our emotions) and what is of our spirit (where Jesus lives and speaks in our hearts).

He divides between our soulish feelings and what He is saying in our spirit.

In learning the leading of the Holy Spirit, God's Word sharpens our spirit to discern when something is stirring our emotions but is not God's leading. Our emotions are not bad. It's just that our emotions can get in the way of the Holy Spirit's leading at times. The other aspect is our mental reasoning. Sometimes our mind reasons away what the Spirit is prompting us to do. This is why we need to train our spirit to hear and obey God's voice.

Chapter 5

Know Your
Spiritual Authority

You are able to use your authority as a Christian when you believe that the Word of God is absolute truth. Today's woke culture wants to question and challenge the truth and authority of the Bible. You have to know what the Bible says about your authority and then decide to believe the Bible even when you don't understand everything in it. You will grow in your understanding, but you have to believe the Bible. We call that *trust*. It is trusting the integrity, justice and overall character of God.

When Jesus was raised from the dead, He gained back the authority for mankind that Adam had lost in the beginning, and He then gave that authority to us (Matthew 28:18–20; Mark 16:16–18). *Authority* in these Scriptures describes someone who has been given the delegated position and power to subdue, drive out and rule over the enemy, Satan, as they are submitted to God's authority. We have authority when we are under authority. Our authority in Jesus Christ is for us to command the devil and his demons to be bound and forbidden to operate in situations we pray for.

One day a Roman centurion came to Jesus asking Him to heal his servant. When Jesus said He would come with him to the house, the centurion said that was not necessary, "I'm a man under authority, and I have authority. Just speak the word only and my servant will be healed." Jesus said that He had not seen such great faith prior to this in all the country. Faith and authority combined bring miracles (Matthew 8:5–10).

Jesus was amazed that this man understood authority and that he connected natural authority with spiritual authority.

Jesus said that He has given us power (authority) over all the enemy and nothing can hurt us (Luke 10:19). Our authority comes from knowing and being convinced that God backs His Word.

Ephesians 1:19–23 tells us that God raised Jesus from the dead and seated Him at His right hand in the heavenly realm above all principality, power, might and dominion and every name that is named; and He put all things under Jesus' feet, or His authority, to give the church, His body, authority in the earth.

Ephesians 2:6 says that while we are here on earth we have been raised up together, spiritually speaking, with Jesus to sit with Him in spiritual authority over the demonic spirits that are influencing people and situations here on earth. We can use our authority over demonic spirits when we believe God's Word has final authority. When we are submitted to God and His Word, we can use His Word to speak into situations to be changed in Jesus' name. (See Mark 11:23.)

Second Corinthians 10:4 tells us that God has given us weapons of our warfare that are not carnal (weak physical weapons), but they are mighty spiritual weapons through God that we can use to pull down strongholds. These weapons are:

The Word of God, sword of Spirit (Ephesians 6:17)

The Name of Jesus (Mark 16:17–18; Acts 4:29–31)

The Power of the Holy Spirit (Acts 1:8; 1 John 4:4)

Prayer of Agreement, agreeing together in prayer (Matthew18:18–20)

Praise and Worship (Acts 16:25–26; 2 Chronicles 20:15–22)

The Blood of Jesus, redemption through His blood (Revelation 12:11; Colossians 1:13–14)

"Plead the blood." I had never heard this statement when I was growing up. However, I later learned it was a statement many Pentecostals used. I asked about the word *plead.* I was told it was not about begging God; it is a term used in the courtroom. When a lawyer pleads a case for the one he is defending, he states the facts in court to prove his client's innocence. When we plead the blood of Jesus, we are stating the fact that the blood of Jesus not only cleansed us of sin but also covers our lives to shelter us from the destroyer spirit.

This is like the children of Israel in Egypt. When the destroyer spirit passed over the land and the firstborn son in every house died, God told Israel to sprinkle the blood of an innocent lamb over their doors. This way the destroyer spirit would pass over their home. When we plead the blood of Jesus, we are saying that the destroyer spirit has to pass over our lives and our loved ones.

Chapter 6

Take God's Armor
for the Victory

In the book of Ephesians, the apostle Paul gives us instructions on how to overcome every plan and plot of the enemy.

10 A final word: Be strong in the Lord and in his mighty power.

11 Put on all of God's armor so that you will be able to stand firm against all strategies of the devil.

12 For we are not fighting against flesh-and-blood enemies, but against evil rulers and authorities of the unseen world, against mighty powers in this dark world, and against evil spirits in the heavenly places.

13 Therefore, put on every piece of God's armor so you will be able to resist the enemy in the time of evil. Then after the battle you will still be standing firm.

14 Stand your ground, putting on the belt of truth and the body armor of God's righteousness.

15 For shoes, put on the peace that comes from the Good News so that you will be fully prepared.

16 In addition to all of these, hold up the shield of faith to stop the fiery arrows of the devil.

17 Put on salvation as your helmet, and take the sword of the Spirit, which is the word of God.

18 Pray in the Spirit at all times and on every occasion. Stay alert and be persistent in your prayers for all believers everywhere. (Ephesians 6:10–18 NLT)

The Belt Is Truth

The first piece of the armor of God that Ephesians 6:14 tells us to put on is the belt of truth. When we put on the armor of God, we are choosing to be people who do not lie but speak the truth and let the truth of God's Word live big on the inside of our hearts.

During New Testament days, the belt of a Roman soldier was put on around the waist to hold his weapons and keep his armor together. This also allowed him to move about freely. Being truthful enables us to move about with confidence because we believe we're now in right standing with God and releasing our faith in Him. It is always best to tell the truth because it will ultimately be revealed. The Scripture tells us that the hidden things will be revealed (Luke 12:2). Living by the truth of God's Word will hold your life together.

In the day Paul the apostle was writing, the people of Ephesus who had become saved had lived according to the ways of the culture around them. It was common for the heathen teachers to say that there are times it is better to lie than to tell the truth. They would say it was because it would be more profitable at times or it would be less hurtful. Having been raised in this loose system of morality, these new converts needed Paul to teach them how to live in the character of Jesus Christ. He instructed them to put away lying and speak the truth to each other (Ephesians 4:25). That instruction is also found in Zechariah 8:16.

Jesus prayed in John17:17 AMP, "Sanctify them in the truth [set them apart for Your purposes, make them holy]; Your word is truth."

We choose to walk in paths of truth. This sets us apart in the world we live in because in this world we are told it is sometimes good to lie. This is not true. God wants to deliver our lives, but we have to become honest before Him. God desires truth in the inward parts of our lives (Psalm 51:6). This is why He calls us to confess our sin to Him. He already knows it; but when we confess it to Him, He sees we don't want it in our lives. He cleanses us from sin and unrighteousness, and He creates a clean heart inside of us.

When we are truthful people we have spiritual freedom. Truth is not relative to circumstances as some have said. Some have said, "What's truth for you may not be truth for me or other people." This is a lie. God's Word is the highest truth; it doesn't compromise to fit into the culture or into situations. Lies destroy people.

Hitler said that if you tell a lie over and over, people will ultimately believe it. That happened during WWII. As many turned their heads away, millions of Jews and mentally disabled people were killed in gas chambers and in other ways. Hitler was an atheist. He believed he could raise up a perfect race of people where he would be ruler. He was deceived. Today we must be cautious to discern news media, social media and people promoting lies: information that does not agree with God's Word.

We are told to bring our lives into submission to obey what God's Word says. God's Word is what sets us free (John 8:31–32). As we continue in it, we will learn freedom in order to live free. Our Founding Fathers of America understood from experience how tyrants will persuade people to believe so they can control and oppress them.

Truth isn't an opinion; it is a person, Jesus Christ. Truth won't always be popular. It takes courage to stand up for God's truth. The more we meditate the truth of God's Word, the more we will keep our lives in submission to His truth.

The Sword Is the Word

God's Word is the sword of the Spirit (Ephesians 6:17). The Romans created a sword that was 19 inches long so it would be easily handled. The tip of the sword was turned upward so it could rip out the insides of the enemy. Both sides of the sword's blade were sharp.

According to Hebrews 4:12, this sword, which is the Word of God, is sharper than any two-edged sword. Rick Renner in his book *Sparkling Gems* points out that one side represents the fact that God spoke the Scripture, and the other side represents the fact that we speak the Scripture and watch the enemy flee.

When a person believes and speaks Scripture, circumstances change. You believe God backs His Word to perform it. When you speak Scripture with faith, you release a weapon against the enemy. And even though the spirit realm is invisible, the words you've spoken attack the spirits of darkness, driving them out of a situation. It is a weapon of offense against the enemy. God's Word, like a sword, is powerful to destroy strongholds of the devil. We overcome the devil by the blood of the Lamb and the Word of our testimony (Revelation 12:11).

One of our former church security officers served in the US military overseas in Iraq and is a sharpshooter. I spoke with him about his experience in the military. He told me that he had to know his weapon so well that he could take his gun apart and put it back together even in the dark. He was told to sleep with it and never let it leave his side. It was as though it became a part of him.

I thought to myself, that is exactly what God wants for us to do with our weapon (the Word of God). He wants us to know how to rightly handle it, to know how to take it apart (study it to understand it) and put it together (to see how it is all connected and know how God wants us to use it in our personal lives). Some people don't know how to rightly handle it. (See 2 Timothy 2:15 AMPC.)

I have used Scripture at various times when I've experienced Satan's attacks. In situations that I didn't know what to do in my natural mind, instead of saying, "I don't know what to do," I would say, "I have the mind of Christ, and He's going to show me what to do or send someone to help me do this."

I remember my first mission trip after my late husband had passed. We had always ministered together, but now I was on my own. I prayed, and God led two people to minister with me—my son-in-law and another young leader in our church. We had a miraculous crusade.

After I returned, my assistant said I had been asked to pray that week at Congress in Washington, D.C. It was Women's Week, and they needed a woman pastor. I prayed and heard the Holy Spirit, in my heart, give me the Scripture to pray. When I prayed, Nancy Pelosi, Speaker of the House at the time, was behind me. We walked out of the room, and I was able to take her hands briefly and pray for her. We, as Christians, are carriers of God's glory; wherever He leads us, we can expect Him to use our lives to impact others.

I did not get to pray the salvation prayer with Nancy Pelosi, but I believe my prayer spoke to her. The man escorting us said to a friend with me, "She never takes this much time with others. It's probably because she's a woman." I believe it was probably because I carried the presence of God, and God was trying to speak to her.

The Word Is an Offensive Weapon

As we mentioned earlier in Chapter 2, Jesus overcame the devil by speaking Scripture. Jesus knew we, as believers, would need to know how to overcome the enemy. Jesus knew the supernatural power of God's Word would stop the enemy; He knew we needed to have this instruction to overcome.

Jesus didn't overcome the devil because He was Almighty God in the flesh on earth; He overcame by believing and speaking the particular Word of God that was needed to respond to each of these temptations. Each Scripture He quoted was related to the temptation Satan was tempting Him with.

Jesus spoke the *rhema* Word of God to counter the devil's attacks. The Greek word *rhema* (revealed) is an inspired spoken Word of God given by the direction of the Holy Spirit. It has supernatural power when we speak it.

The Holy Spirit wants to quicken a particular Scripture, a *rhema*, to us when we are fighting against the enemy. He wants to quicken a word in our heart to speak in the situation to change things. We know all of Scripture has power, but when the Holy Spirit quickens a Scripture to us to use in prayer, we have tapped into God's supernatural intervention.

The Scripture that God gives us to speak, the *rhema*, pierces through the enemy's lies, his negative thoughts and his accusations. As we speak what God's Word says, the enemy gets tired after a while and he retreats for a time.

A man in our church who had a bipolar personality had been on medications, and sometimes he was like a zombie. He had been prayed for by many different people. He wasn't living a full abundant life. He decided one day that he was going to apply the Word that he had heard over the years by speaking Scripture over himself daily (like taking medicine). He shared how one day it dawned on him that he was healed, and he didn't need the medication. From then on he continued declaring what God had said about him to remain healed.

Another situation was a girl who had epileptic seizures. Her dad decided he was going to speak Scripture over her life daily. He asked her doctor if he would reduce her medication. The doctor agreed and said if they did not see any improvement they could always increase the medication again. Right before she was totally healed she had about 200 seizures in one day. Her dad, in a state of desperation over the devil's all-out attack, spoke the Scripture about her healing in prayer. He commanded the devil to stop and declared she was the seed of the righteous and was delivered in Jesus' name. (See Proverbs 11:21.)

She was healed and has shared her testimony here and in other countries. It has encouraged people that God created us, and He can fix us. Nothing is impossible with

Him. That was several years ago, and she hasn't had any more seizures. I felt that her dad's determined faith was crucial in her healing. The father is the authority in the home, and he would not let go of his faith. He kept his own life right with God, and he was declaring what God had said.

We Chose to Stand

When our daughter Ruthie was a baby, she became very ill. That was at the same time that we were first starting our church. It was a testing time in many ways. We were speaking Scripture over our lives and over our kids for God's protection and health. I took her to the doctor for a checkup, and the doctor was led by the Holy Spirit to draw blood from her because of a concern.

I returned home and the doctor, who was a Christian, called me. He said, "I have to give you a possible medical report, but I'm going to also give you the report of the Lord." He proceeded to tell me to take her to the hospital where he would meet us and that the possible diagnosis was spinal meningitis, a rare type of pneumonia, or leukemia. Her white count was very high. Then he said, "But the report of the Lord says, 'By His [Jesus'] stripes she was healed. She's the seed of the righteous, and she is delivered in Jesus' name.'" And he added that he would call my husband at work.

My husband and I went to the hospital, praying in the Spirit and speaking Scripture over Ruthie. We did not talk the negative report. We only asked one other person to stay in faith in prayer with us. As the doctors took tests, they immediately ruled out meningitis and pneumonia. They were not sure, however, about the leukemia because of the high white count. She was in the hospital for a few days, and then we brought her home.

We kept speaking Scripture over her. We thanked the other doctors who were brought in on the case, but we would not agree with any negative report. One doctor said to our doctor, "These people are very positive." Yes, when you stand in faith, you choose to believe God's Word. Over the next ten months, I had to bring her to a clinic every week to be checked. I got to know everyone who worked there.

We had received a prophetic word spoken by a woman in ministry over Ruthie a few weeks before about her being healed. She did not know anything about Ruthie nor did she know what she had been going through. We watched God bring her white count down over those next ten months, and she was totally healed.

Today, she is still healed at 42 years old. She is married and has three children; she and her husband are pastors of a church. Someone might say, "Why did it take so long?" I don't know everything; but I know there was a spiritual battle going on for her destiny, and we chose to stand in faith and believe God's Word.

Overpower Wrong Thoughts With Words

Several years ago a friend of ours in our church shared that he struggled with pornography. He said that he thought once he married he would not be harassed by it, but it continued to harass him. He began to drink alcohol, as well. It started to affect his marriage.

He decided he needed to admit he had a problem and asked his wife and a friend to be his accountability partners and took Scriptures to speak and put them on cards. He also was involved in a small men's discipleship group at church. He became free as he believed the Word of God and spoke it. Since that time, he has mentored other men and encouraged them that God's Word is supernatural and can deliver a person from anything when they believe it, speak it and act upon it.

Chapter 7

Speak to Your Mountain

Jesus said to His disciples in Mark 11:22–24 NKJV, "Have faith in God. For assuredly, I say to you, whoever says to this mountain, 'Be removed and be cast into the sea,' and does not doubt in his heart, but believes that those things he says will be done, he will have whatever he says." Speak to whatever is in your way; whatever problem or obstacle that is before you, speak to it and believe as you speak that what you say will come to pass. It will happen.

Faith speaks! The spirit of faith is "I believe, therefore I speak" (2 Corinthians 4:13). The Bible gives us many examples of this principle.

- God spoke this world into existence (Genesis 1:3–26; Hebrews 11:3).

- God told Ezekiel to speak to dry bones to live, and they came to life (Ezekiel 37).

- His angels hearken to the voice of His Word (Psalm 103:20). You might ask, "Who gives voice to His

Word?" You and I do. When we speak God's Word with faith, angels go to see that that Word is activated.

- "You will also declare a thing and it will be established for you" (Job 22:28 NKJV).

- "I will say of the Lord, He is my refuge and my fortress: my God; in Him will I trust" (Psalm 91:2).

The first time I heard this teaching about speaking God's Word, I began memorizing Psalm 91 and speaking it over my life. I went out jogging in the street one day with a friend. She was way ahead of me, and I could not see her any longer. Suddenly, a man came out of his house with a gun pointed straight at me. My mind couldn't think quickly enough to know what to do, but I started quoting Psalm 91 as I ran away. I heard the click of the gun, but it obviously had no bullets.

My friend came back around, and I asked her about the man. She told me he had been shell-shocked in the Vietnam War, and his parents kept him locked up inside the house. I told her he got out that day, but Psalm 91 delivered me. Praise God! I was more cautious after that, but I saw the power of speaking God's Word working on my behalf. My angels were with me and delivered me.

When we first began Victory as a church, we did what other churches did at that time; we went to take out a loan at a bank to buy property for our church. The Lord had led us to a former car lot business that was for sale. It was being carried by three different banks that said they would go together, and we would get the loan from one bank.

The day before the deal was to happen my husband came home from work and said we needed to come into the power of agreement. One bank president said he was backing out of the deal. My husband took my hand and said, "We've already started moving into the facility, and we have to have it. We agree that this particular bank president will either change his mind before noon tomorrow or he will be moved to a better situation for us all." This was speaking to the mountain to move.

The next day when our administrative staff person called that bank and asked to speak to the president, the lady who answered said, "I'm sorry. He's not in."

When asked, "When will he be in," she said, "Well, as of yesterday he no longer is president here. Would you like to speak to the president?" Our administrator replied, "Yes."

Needless to say, God moved him out of the way for our deal to go through. We were not praying against the man. We prayed for him to have a better situation if that was how God wanted to work through our prayer.

Chapter 8

Keep Digging

In John 8:31–32 Jesus tells His disciples, "If ye continue in my word, then are ye my disciples indeed; and ye shall know the truth, and the truth shall make you free." *To continue* is to not quit. Even when you know a lot already, God's Word always has fresh revelation for you, and you are learning stability for future testing time.

Over the years, my time of daily reading and studying the Bible has produced stability in my life. As I have walked through various tests, I've experienced God's supernatural support and His insights.

I remember in those early years I wasn't sure if anything was changing in me from my reading. One day I asked the Lord, "Is anything happening in me?" I couldn't see the growth although I realized later it was happening. When a seed is planted in the ground, you don't dig it up to see if it's growing. You can't see it, but it is growing underneath the dirt that has covered it. I heard the Lord say in my heart, "Continue reading daily; I'm producing stability in you because you will need it in the days ahead."

The definition of *stability* is "not likely to fall or give way; firmly establish, able to continue, unwavering, not subject to emotional instability; able to react to a disturbing force by maintaining."

Storms of life will come because we live in a fallen world and we have an enemy, Satan. Jesus said, "In the world you have tribulation and trials and distress and frustration; but be of good cheer [take courage; be confident, certain, undaunted]! For I have overcome the world" (John 16:33 AMPC).

In 1989, I went to an International Women in Leadership meeting attended by a small number of women leaders. I was probably the youngest leader there. I led the worship a cappella. A lady came up to me who was prophetic. She asked me to tell her my testimony, which I did. She said, "Your foundation is good, but dig deeper. The days are coming when ministers will fall like flies, but the Lord showed me you would not fall. You'll remain fixed or settled, but dig deeper."

As I pondered that word, another well-known woman in leadership came to me and gave me a similar word. I continued to think about the word and asked the Lord what it meant to dig deeper because I thought I was doing all I knew to do in my walk with Him.

Then another woman I knew, who was a strong intercessory prayer person, came and asked me what the others had said. I told her. She began telling me about a time when she and her husband were building a home outside of the city where they lived. They had to dig a well for water in their area.

The man digging the well told her and her husband that he could dig to the first rock bed level and they would have water; however, in a time of a drought, they would not have enough supply. In that case, they would have to haul water from the city to their home. He said he could dig to the second rock bed level and they would always have water even during a drought, but it would cost more. Her husband immediately said to go ahead and dig to the second rock bed level.

She was not happy. She said, "But that is going to take my money we had set aside for curtains and flooring for the house."

Her husband would not budge from his position, and the man dug to the second rock bed level. Almost two years later, after they had moved into the house, a drought hit their area. Their home and one other home were the only two that had water among the 20 homes that had been built.

At this time I heard the Lord say to me, "What do you do when you dig a hole in the backyard to plant a bush? Do you do anything different, or do you just keep doing what you're doing as you dig the hole deeper?" I realized I needed to keep doing what I was doing in seeking God and growing in my relationship with Him.

There are many times people start reading with great enthusiasm and discipline, but over time they quit. They feel they can coast on what they've read. Luke 18:8 AMPC asks, "When the Son of Man comes, will He find [persistence in] faith on the earth?"

When Jesus returns will He find persistent faith? *Persistent* means "continuing without change; persevering to continue in a course of action in spite of difficulty, obstacles, discouragement or opposition." Even when you feel like you've grown a lot and you've experienced a lot from God's Word, don't quit.

Years later I experienced God's grace and stability supporting my life when my husband passed into eternity at age 57. I wasn't expecting him to leave at that time. But I felt God's support and stability to continue. I heard God say, "For me to live is Christ, and to die is gain" (Philippians 1:21). He spoke to my heart, "Billy Joe lived for Me and now he has gained. He has entered into his rest and the rewards of his labor on earth. He fulfilled his purpose, but your purpose has not changed. You are still called to minister and pastor people."

Then the Lord spoke to my heart that I needed to speak to our congregation the next weekend, so I did. The board then asked me to pastor, and I knew in my spirit I was to do that; but He told me I would be an interim pastor and transition to my son later. I watched God work in a divine way during this time.

Chapter 9

Encourage Yourself

"Let us not become weary in doing good, for at the proper time we will reap a harvest if we do not give up" (Galatians 6:9 NIV).

There are "antichrist spirits" in our world who are against Christ and against His people—you and me. The antichrist spirit that is in this world seeks to wear down the saints (Daniel 7:25). This is one of the characteristics that the Antichrist will have when he comes on the scene. Right now the world is being influenced by that spirit. We each have to know ourselves and know what the Holy Spirit is telling us to do and not to do.

Second Peter 2:7–8 tells us that Lot was "vexed" or worn down, distressed and tormented by the conversations and lifestyles of the wicked around him. Then verse 9 says that God can rescue the godly from various testing situations and hold the unrighteous accountable. Believers must take strength from spending time with the Lord and stand up against the spirits of this world that seek to wear them down.

Daniel 11:32 MSG tells us that in the end time "those who stay courageously loyal to their God will take a strong stand."

Scripture encourages us when we need it. The psalmist said he had been lied about and malicious accusations had been told about him. He wrote, "I would have lost heart, unless I had believed that I would see the goodness of the Lord in the land of the living" (Psalm 27:13 NKJV).

Over the years, there have been times that we've been lied about, but the Lord has dealt with me to keep my mind fixed on God's Word in order to stay in faith. I've had to not look at the comments of the media and the social media in order to keep my conversation in faith. Many times the Holy Spirit has directed me to keep my mouth shut, especially around certain people. Staying in faith requires self-control and meditation on God's Word instead of circumstances. It means not talking your thoughts but trusting God to work. This is how to stay in faith.

There are times we must encourage ourselves by speaking Scripture to ourselves. One time in the beginning of our pastoring, around 1982, we were going through a very difficult trial; and as I was spending time with the Lord, I asked Him to cause someone to call me that day and encourage me. Instead, He spoke to me very strongly in my heart: "David encouraged himself in the Lord" (1 Samuel 30:6).

I knew that was when David had returned with his mighty men to their village of Ziklag and discovered that while they were gone their houses were burned and their wives and children had been taken. Those men who had been committed to David suddenly began to speak of stoning him.

I'm sure David felt thoughts of disappointment that while he was doing what he believed was right to do, his men were robbed by the enemy. He then had to face thoughts of fear listening to his men's conversations. But "David encouraged himself in the Lord his God." David sought the Lord and asked Him what to do. The Lord told him to go after them and he would recover all. They did, and they recovered all that the enemy had taken.

I encouraged myself as I spent time with the Lord and the Scripture. Later that same day, I received two phone calls from people I did not expect to hear from. One was a young guy who had been in our youth group years before. He didn't know anything we were walking through. He said, "I just felt to call you and say that your fruit remains in my life." Wow! I had not known what had happened to him, so it was very encouraging to me that he was still serving the Lord. The other call was from a friend who just felt to call me, also not knowing anything that we were going through, just to encourage me. God didn't have to do that, but He showed me that He cared and that He was involved in my life.

In another similar testing time years later, the Lord gave me a song to write called "I'm Gonna Take It Back."

I felt in prayer that we were being led by the Holy Spirit to take back what the devil had stolen. This brought strength to me that I needed. God told me to keep my heart in the love of God. Let go of the past. Keep my mind meditating His Scripture and not talk about anyone else. He told me He would work in the lives of others.

Proverbs 24:10 says,

- "If you faint in the day of adversity, Your strength is small" (NKJV).

- "If you give up when trouble comes, it shows that you are weak" (NCV).

I am continuing still today. I still read my Bible through each year; I teach, study, pray and write. I pastored for five years after my husband passed and then transitioned the church to my son Paul and his wife, Ashley. I continue to minister weekly. I travel in ministry, oversee prayer at our church, and teach in our Bible college. I am grateful that my son and his wife pastor our church raising up this generation doing the work of ministry. I am also grateful that my other children and their spouses are serving in full-time ministry impacting the world around them. We have all continued in what we know to do from the Lord.

Jesus stated that to be His disciple (His follower), a person had to continue in His Word. "If ye continue in my word, then are ye my disciples indeed; and ye shall know the truth, and the truth shall make you free" (John 8:31–32).

I've known people who were delivered from drugs or alcohol or sexual sin by separating themselves from the problem and then declaring what God's Word says instead of what their desires or feelings said. They chose to cast down wrong imaginations and bring their thoughts and desires captive to what God's Word says. The Word of God sanctifies us (John 17:17); it sets us apart from the sin and consecrates us to God.

Chapter 10

How to Get Guidance Through God's Word

God's Word is a lamp to our feet and a light to show us the path He wants us on (Psalm 119:105). It may not say, "Go to Dallas, Texas"; however, it will give you peace or lack of peace about directions you are to take or not to take in life.

Colossians 3:15 AMPC says, "Let the peace (soul harmony which comes) from Christ rule (act as umpire continually) in your hearts [deciding and settling with finality all questions that arise in your minds, in that peaceful state]." After you've prayed about what to do, listen for peace on the inside. If you don't have peace, don't make a move. The umpire in a ballgame calls the calls whether someone is safe or out. Let God's peace make the call whether something is God's will or your own thoughts or someone else's desire for your life.

God wants to use His Word to guide us in life. The Bible gives principles that enable us to hear the voice of the Holy Spirit on the inside of our hearts helping us make right decisions. The more we take time to learn the Word of God the more we gain better discernment in decision-making.

I remember when my feelings were saying to me to quit school and just get married. But then one night as I was reading in my Bible, my eyes fell upon Luke 14:28–33. This Scripture speaks about not starting to build a tower or going out to war before counting the cost so that whatever a person starts they make sure they can finish.

I heard that little voice in my spirit (a strong thought) that told me I was to finish my college degree at ORU. (This would be important one year later after my husband and I were married.) The Lord spoke in my heart, "You believed to be here at ORU, and I made the provision. No person starts to build a tower or goes out to battle without first counting the cost and making sure they can finish building the house and meet whatever army they are going to meet and overcome. You will finish ORU." At that moment I stopped thinking about quitting and started thinking about finishing strong. We got married the following summer while I was a junior and Billy Joe was a senior in college.

When Billy Joe graduated, he prayed about three possibilities for us: (1) move to Colorado to go with Youth For Christ, (2) go to work with another ministry out of state working with youth, (3) remain in Tulsa to work as a youth pastor at a church. I told him what God had said to me about graduating at ORU.

He replied, "Well, you can stay here, and I'm going to obey God."

I said, "Well, we're married. I'm going to be with you."

Then I prayed, "Lord, You'll have to speak to him."

Within a couple of days he said, "I can't shake the church offer here in Tulsa." So he called that church to check on the position. The pastor said, "You're the only one who applied. Why don't you come, and after two months if we like you and you like us, you can stay?"

The youth group tripled within two months. The pastor saw kids coming who had been away from God for a long time, and he asked us to stay. I finished my degree at ORU while working on staff at this church.

We had prayed when we took this job that God would put us where we could get our doctrine straight. That summer Brother Kenneth Hagin announced he was starting Rhema Bible School that next month. The pastor of the church said, "Start it here." So Brother Hagin did. We were able to get the teaching of the Word of Faith because of this. Sometimes words from the Lord get tested to see if we are willing to do whatever God says and willing to flow with Him.

In 1982, a woman in our church had prophesied about the doors of the Soviet Union opening and that ministers would go across the Soviet Union like huge combines reaping a harvest of souls. Then she said, "And your pastor will be one of them."

About 1987, my late husband heard in his spirit to translate his little book, *This New Life,* into the Russian language. He had written it for new converts. At that time we did not know any Russians in our city or area. But soon God led a couple from Canada to move to Tulsa and enroll in our Victory Bible College. The man's parents were Russian, so he had grown up speaking both English and Russian.

The Russian president Mikhail Gorbachev was put in office as the leader of the Soviet Union after his mentor had been assassinated. He established what was called "perestroika" and "glasnost," a plan to open up the Soviet Union to the West. And just like the prophetic word that had been spoken, we were a part of a huge spiritual group of combines going in and reaping a harvest of people being saved.

When we returned from our first trip in August 1991, God gave my husband two Scriptures about going back to Russia each month to hold weeklong meetings. The Scriptures were: Isaiah 52:5–7 and Acts 18:9–11.

We knew it would be 18 months and that we were not to move there but to go there each month preaching, teaching and demonstrating the Word of God with signs and wonders. Thousands were saved, and we were able to give out 1.5 million Bibles and books to the people who came at that time from the eleven time zones of the former Soviet Union. Many went back to where they were from to start churches and Bible groups.

Chapter 11

Think According to the Word
(Renewing Your Mind)

It's easy to see that sometimes we don't think correctly. The world tells us that we are whatever we think. The Bible says that as a man thinks, so is he (Proverbs 23:7).

If we think we are unable, unqualified, insufficient, hopeless or a failure, then we won't do certain things. If a person thinks on pornography, lying, committing sex outside of marriage, drinking, gambling, etc., they will at some time act that out. This is why we have to renew our minds to what the Bible says about us.

Every person in the Bible who was used by God had to deal with negative thoughts at times—especially feeling inadequate, fearing failure and questioning how God could still use them. Consider Moses, who felt misunderstood. He ran away after killing a man because he was trying to help those who were oppressed.

Think of David who, after he had won many wars, sinned with Bathsheba. He had turmoil in his family. Later, he was hunted down by a son who wanted to kill him. Yet God said David was a man after His own heart (Acts 13:22).

Think of Abram who lied about Sarah, saying she was his sister when, in reality, she was his half-sister and she was his wife. Yet, God called him the friend of God and the father of our faith (James 2:23; Romans 4:16).

Then there's Rahab, the harlot, who not only changed her belief to trust in God, but also quit her former life and married a Jewish man, later being in the genealogy of Jesus (Matthew 1:5). Still, God chose to use each of them.

They had to believe in the mercy of God, and they had to believe He wanted to use their lives. They also had to keep their minds on His Word to them. Abraham didn't have the written Word of God, so he had to rely on the word God spoke to him—and God did not speak to him very often. He followed whatever he heard God say. Moses was the one who received the Word of God and wrote it for the people of Israel.

Israel had the Torah (the first five books written of the Old Testament). Later other books were written under the Old Covenant (Old Testament). The New Testament Gospels and the book of Acts were written by disciples of Jesus: Matthew, Mark, Luke and John. The letters were written by the apostles: Paul, Peter, James, Jude and John.

In the New Testament, we realize we are saved by faith in the blood of Jesus. However, in order to grow spiritually and see God work, we have to renew our minds to what God's Word says.

Chapter 12

Empower Your Destiny

I met a young woman, Tatum, who had moved to Tulsa in 2015. She told me her story.

She was living with her boyfriend and working at a restaurant. Some time earlier, she had gone to jail because of drugs. She had gotten pregnant and lost the baby. Tatum became friends with a girl at the restaurant where she worked. The girl, who was a Christian, invited her to our church during our annual conference.

Tatum was discouraged with her life; but when she walked into the church service, she felt something so tangible that she wanted it. She got saved and said that she immediately wanted to learn the Bible.

On a whim, her friend said she should apply for the scholarship to the Bible college—so she did. She thought, Lord, I have no money, so if You want me to go, You will have to provide. The next night she won the scholarship drawing. She was so surprised and elated that she let out curse words and cried. Her friend was also excited and said, "Why don't you apply for Victory College housing?" She applied and got into the housing. This moved her away from the wrong setting she was living in.

Once she was in Bible college, she was being healed and restored every week, and her eyes were being opened to truth. She shared how God was removing one thing at a time from her life that she needed to have changed.

She worked at Camp Victory for five summers. After completing VBC, she attended community college and graduated from ORU with a Bachelor of Arts degree in Writing and English Literature. She served under Terry and Brenda Henshaw, writing grants for City Serve Ministry, who've helped so many people,

Tatum met her husband at Victory. He had been a meth addict and alcoholic but had gotten saved and transformed by God's Spirit. He worked at Victory for a season, and they married. They now live in Texas and are involved in ministry there.

When we renew our minds to the Word of God, we open up our lives for God to transform our lives personally and for Him to use us to bring His transforming power to others. She is walking in the destiny God had for her all along. She just didn't know it. The more we put God's Word in our lives, the more He reveals His will, His plans and His gifts that He has given to us to use for His kingdom.

Chapter 13

Prepare for Eternity

Eternity is ahead for every person. Life does not end at physical death. We will either go to heaven or hell. God created us and loves us, but He gave us a free will to choose where we will go one day.

"[God] has planted eternity in the human heart, but even so, people cannot see the whole scope of God's work from beginning to end" (Ecclesiastes 3:11 NLT).

"So we look not at the things which are seen, but at the things which are unseen; for the things which are visible are temporal [just brief and fleeting], but the things which are invisible are everlasting and imperishable" (2 Corinthians 4:18 AMP).

We choose to live our lives in view of eternity. This is why we choose to not hold onto sin, not hold onto past hurts or grievous things, not hold onto grief and disappointments and instead allow God to work in our lives here on earth.

I remember a friend of mine who was overcoming cancer said to me, "It's not worth holding offences." She had carried some things where her family had felt mistreated in a situation. She felt that her resentment opened the door to the cancer. She said, "It's not worth it."

God's Word is eternal, so we choose to live by the Word of God. We do not live by the circumstances around us that we can see. Circumstances are temporal. That means they are temporary and they can change. When we believe and declare what God's Word says, our faith is in Him instead of what the news media or others say, or what it looks like.

God's Word tells us we will ultimately go to either heaven or hell at death. We prepare for eternity by believing and accepting Jesus as our Lord and Savior, living our lives in surrender to Him and letting go of wrongs we have experienced. We prepare by doing things that help us grow spiritually: God's Word, prayer, attending church, fellowshipping with other believers, giving out of our lives, and worshiping Him.

We can live our lives here on earth making a difference in peoples' lives and helping others come to know the Lord. Then when we step into eternity, we will hear God say, "Well done, good and faithful servant…Enter into the joy of the Lord" (Matthew 25:23 NKJV).

The Bible tells us that eternity is very real. We don't cease to exist when we die. We move from earth to another location. The Bible records a true story regarding this that happened before Jesus died and was raised from the dead.

Jesus told this story about two men who died. One man, Lazarus, went to Abraham's bosom (an upper level of hell where the righteous went before Jesus died and was raised from the dead), and the other man went to the lowest hell. The one in the lowest hell could still feel, see, and talk. He was thirsty and tormented in the flames of hell. He called out to Abraham asking him to have the other man dip his finger in water and touch his tongue. Abraham replied, "I can't because there is a great gulf between us that cannot be passed over."

The man then said, "Have Lazarus go back and warn my brothers so they won't come here."

Abraham told him, "They have the Scripture of Moses and the prophets. If they won't believe the Word of God, they won't be persuaded if someone rises from the dead to speak to them." (See Luke 16:19–31.)

People will still be able to see, feel, and communicate in eternity. Some people have tried to say that people die like a dog and don't exist anymore after death, but that is not true. Hell is not one big party either. Hell is a place of suffering, pain, torment, heartache and great thirst. Hell is an eternal burning furnace; it is utter darkness where there will be weeping and gnashing of teeth (Matthew 25:30). Jesus said that hell will be a place of everlasting punishment (Matthew 25:46). He said not to fear those who can kill the body but fear him who is able to destroy both soul and body in hell (Matthew 10:28).

Revelation 21:8 NLT says, "Cowards, unbelievers, the corrupt, murderers, the immoral, those who practice witchcraft, idol worshipers, and all liars—their fate is in the fiery lake of burning sulfur. This is the second death."

We don't have to go to hell. No matter how bad you have been, you can repent and receive the cleansing blood of Jesus Christ, and you can be free. Then you can go to heaven when you die.

Jesus' resurrection made the way for us to go to heaven. He told the disciples He was going to prepare a place for them and for us (John 14:3). Heaven is a beautiful place. People will enter into a rest from their labors and will experience God's rewards. We will know each other, and we will experience His love, His joy, and His peace forever. We will have glorified bodies, and we will celebrate His presence and victory.

Chapter 14

Examine the Evidence

What if someone challenges you questioning, "How do you know that the Word of God is true?" One thing for sure, you cannot argue with someone's testimony who has believed God's Word and experienced the miracle power of it.

God's Word is not just words. The Word of God is supernatural. It has healed people, set people free from addictions, delivered people from tragedies and accidents, and brought provision to people. It is alive and powerful (Hebrews 4:12). You can't argue with people's testimonies.

Jesus and His Word are one. You cannot receive His salvation and reject His Word. John 18:37 NKJV tells us that when Jesus was questioned by Pilate, He said, "For this cause I have come into the world, that I should bear witness to the truth. Everyone who is of the truth hears My voice."

Sometimes people question, "Doesn't the Word of God contradict itself?" No! Those who read it with an attitude of doubt and unbelief will find things to argue about. When you read it from the perspective of belonging and living in surrender to God's supernatural grace in your life, you see how God answers your questions and fits it all together.

Even though the Bible was written over a 1600-year period by 40 different authors who wrote 66 books, the writers had a consistent viewpoint of life and set of facts. They include the following:

(1) where we came from—as a special creation of God

(2) why we are here—to serve and glorify God

(3) where we (as eternal beings) are going—eternity and facing eternal judgment.[1]

I realize many religions say that their book is truth: the *Koran* (Islam's book), the *Book of Mormon,* the Hindus *Bhagavad Gita* all claim to be the source of truth. Karl Marx, an atheist who detested the Bible, claimed his writing of the *Communist Manifesto* was the ultimate truth. It's interesting to see that although these books have actually used portions of Scripture and put it in their own words, none of these books have produced the saving good fruit that the Bible has produced. Their theories have been proven to be oppressive to the people who embraced their teachings.

History Validates Bible Prophecies

The Bible contains hundreds of prophecies that already have been fulfilled. Look at the following:

- Israel's rebirth as a nation was prophesied in 600 BC (Isaiah 66:8–9; Ezekiel 37:1–14). For almost 2000 years since AD 70 the nation of Israel did not exist. Then on May 15,1948, Israel became a nation. In 1967 (Six-Day War), its area quadrupled, and Jerusalem became Jewish property again.

- Ezekiel, who lived around 550 BC, prophesied that the city of Tyre (Tyrus, a little island close to Lebanon, in the Mediterranean, formerly a Phoenician city in ancient times) would be destroyed years before it happened. Nebuchadnezzar attacked it, then Alexander attacked it; it was destroyed by 322 BC (Ezekiel 26:3–5).

- One-hundred-and-fifty years before the birth of the Persian King Cyrus, Isaiah prophesied that he would be born, he would be king and he would subdue nations. Gates would not be shut but would open before him. History records that following Cyrus' destruction of Babylon in 539 BC the empire never recovered (Isaiah 45:1–3).[2]

- The prophecies of Isaiah and Jeremiah concerning the destruction of Babylon, Edom, and Nineveh, cities that had set themselves against Israel, were fulfilled over 2500 years ago.

  Babylon was destroyed 539 BC (Isaiah 14:22; Jeremiah 25:12).

  Edom was destroyed sixth century BC (Obadiah 1:1,8).

  Nineveh was destroyed 612 BC (Nahum 3:1–7).[3]

Jesus' Life Fulfilled Prophecies

(No other religion's leader has had this happen.) Over hundreds of years, even over a thousand years before He came to earth, prophecies were given regarding His birth, rejection, death and resurrection. (*indicates fulfilled*)

- He was to be born in Bethlehem, Micah 5:2. (*Matthew 2:1–6; Luke 2:4–5,7,15)

- He would be born of a virgin, Genesis 3:15; Isaiah 7:14. (*Matthew 1:18–25)

- He would be a prophet, Deuteronomy 18:15. (*John 7:40–42; Acts 3:20–23)

- He would ride a donkey into Jerusalem, Zechariah 9:9. (*John 12:12–16)

- He would be rejected by His own, Isaiah 53:1–3. (*John 1:10–11; 12:37–38)

- He would be betrayed by one of His own, Psalm 41:9; Psalm 55:12–13. (*Luke 22:21–22; John 13:18,21,26)

- He would be betrayed for 30 pieces of silver, Zechariah 11:12–13. (*Matthew 26:14–16; 27:3)

- He would be silent before His accusers, Isaiah 53:7. (*Mark 15:3–5)

- He would be spit upon, mocked and beaten, Isaiah 50:6; Psalm 22:6–7. (*Matthew 26:67–68; Mark 15:19)

- He would be crucified, pierced in His hands and feet, Psalm 22:14–16; Zechariah12:10. (*Mark 15:20; John 19:15–16)

- He would suffer with sinners, Isaiah 53:12. (*Matthew 27:38; Luke 23:32–33)

- His garments would be divided by casting lots, Psalm 22:18. (*Mark 15:24; John 19:24)

- None of Jesus' bones would be broken, Numbers 9:12. (*John 19:33)

- He would be buried in a rich man's tomb, Isaiah 53:9. (*Matthew 27:57–60)

- He would rise from the dead, Psalm 16:10; Psalm 30:3. (*Mark 16:6; Acts 2:27–32)

Archeology Confirms the Bible

- In 1868, Frederick Augustus Klein, a missionary in Jerusalem, discovered a large tablet in Dhiban, Jordan, dated to the ninth century BC. The message, written in the Moabite language, began with the statement, "I am Mesha, son of Kemos-yatti, King of Moab." This king continued to write about a war fought with Israel in 850 BC when Moab revolted against King Jehoram of Israel. The writings on the stone agree with the biblical history in 2 Kings 3. The Mesha Stele is on display in the Louvre in Paris, France.[4]

- In 1872, Assyrian tablets were discovered with a story identical to the narrative in Genesis 6–9. George Smith, a British assyriologist, discovered an Assyrian account of the flood on one of the twelve tablets, called the Epic of Gilgamesh, stored in the British Museum from excavations of mid-seventh century BC Nineveh.[5]

- In 1867, British engineer and archeologist Charles Warren discovered an underground shaft cut in bedrock. It was King Hezekiah's tunnel. Prior to the Assyrian invasion of Judah 701BC, King Hezekiah ordered a tunnel to be made under the city of David to bring the waters of Gihon Spring to the southwestern side of the city (2 Kings 20:20; 2 Chronicles 32:30).[6]

- In the 1930s, Dr. John Garstang, a British archeologist, discovered remains of the walls at Jericho that fell to attackers, falling outward. Later in 1990, *Time* magazine carried an article stating that archeologist Kathleen Kenyon said the remains of Jericho looked as if its walls fell suddenly. The archeologist stated that it appeared also the walls fell outward as if they had been knocked down from inside instead of how walls normally would have been knocked down (Joshua 6:20).[7]

- In the 1930s, J. L. Starkey excavated the site at the ancient city of Lachish. He discovered clay ostracon with letters in carbon ink on the pottery shreds that dated back to 589/588 BC when the Babylonians, under the rule of Nebuchadnezzar, burned the city (Jeremiah 34:7).[8]

- In 1947, the greatest archeological find of the 20th century is attributed to shepherds. They stumbled upon a cave near the Dead Sea that had document fragments mostly written in Hebrew. Similar caves were discovered in the next few years. Of the over 800 fragmentary documents discovered, 190 were from biblical scrolls, and fragments of almost every Old Testament book were found. A complete scroll of Isaiah was also found. The Dead Sea scrolls dated back to the first three centuries BC.[9]

- In 1993, excavators at Tel Dan (northern Israel) uncovered an inscription of letters BTDWD, meaning "House of David," dating back to King David's lineage in the ninth century BC, giving historical credibility to King David's existence.[10]

Chapter 15

Why Read the Bible Anyway?

When we read the Bible, it brings a sense of satisfaction that something supernatural is happening in our lives. We grow by reading and studying and doing what we learn.

- If we want to be His disciple, we're told by Jesus to continue in His Word (John 8:31).

  A disciple is someone who accepts the Bible as their doctrine of belief to follow after Jesus and apply what they've learned. A disciple spreads the belief to others.

- When we continue in God's Word, we learn the truth, and the truth sets us free from anything that Satan would try to bind our lives with (John 8:32).

  One man I met years ago told me that after returning from the Vietnam War, he had been strung out on the drug heroin for a few years. He made a decision to fast and pray and read his

Bible to be free. He did this "cold turkey," and he got free. He never went back to the drugs again.

As we read the Word of God, it reads us and shows us areas we need to change, and then it empowers us to change. The Holy Spirit uses the Word of God to transform our minds and transform our lives.

- We read the Word of God in order to grow spiritually. The Word of God says for us to be rooted and built up in Jesus, to be strengthened spiritually and to walk out what we read (Colossians 2:6–10).

  We can't walk like Him if we don't know His ways and His thoughts. The Bible shows us His ways and shows us the way He thinks about things (Isaiah 55:8–11).

  His ways and thoughts are higher than ours, which means they are better. It doesn't mean they are so high we can't reach them. It means they are better. They bring fruitfulness in our lives. As we read and begin to memorize Scripture, it gets inside of us. When we speak what the Word says, it will not return to God void or without results. It will bring God's will that we are speaking to pass in the earth.

  God's Word will help us not become deceived (Colossians 2:4). As we read the Word of God with an open heart to God, the Holy Spirit opens the eyes of our understanding to understand God's truth.

- God's Word shines a light on our thoughts to hear what God is wanting to say to us. His Word is a lamp to our feet and a light to our path (Psalm 119:105).

- God's Word brings healing to our lives.

    He sent His Word to heal us and to deliver us from all destruction (Psalm 107:20; Proverbs 4:22). When we read God's Word it brings quickening restoration to our lives (Psalm 119:107).

- When we read God's Word, it's like reading a love letter. He tells us His thoughts, and He assures us of His love for us.

    When my late husband and I dated before we were married, we would write letters to each other. I read and reread his letters to me. God's Word is like that. He loves us and wants to communicate with us.

- When we read God's Word, it is a refuge for us and a shield. It is a source of hope (Psalm119:114).

    When I pastored our church after my husband passed away, one year we walked through a difficult test. Instead of reading any newspaper, I read the Bible. It kept my mind focused on right counsel. I believe God protected us and gave us favor and understanding with people during that time. Today many people read social media and their minds become filled with worry, confusion, fear, doubt and unbelief. God's Word gives us stability, peace and confident assurance that He is working on our behalf.

- When we read God's Word, it changes us and transforms us into His image in order for us to do His will instead of conforming to this world system around us (Romans 12:2).

  This world is seeking to conform people to an anti-Christ, anti-biblical mindset. There are those who want all nations to become a one-world socialist government, controlled by the government. God seeks to transform our thinking to think according to the Word of God and respond with that Word instead of responding with our emotions or responding with what other people say.

- When we read and memorize Scripture, we are sharpening our sword to fight against the devil and destroy his thoughts (Ephesians 6:17).

  His Word has power not just in our thoughts, but it has power when we speak it into the atmosphere to change things.

  Jesus used Scripture by speaking it in Matthew 4 each time the devil came to tempt Him and the devil left Him.

Proverbs 18:21 tells us that, "Death and life are in the power of the tongue." We experience the results of our words. When we submit to God's authority and we speak the Scripture, Satan has to obey. We have the greater One living inside of us.

Jesus is greater inside of us than the devil in the world (1 John 4:4).

- When we read the Bible, we will understand what is going on with the world around us. Bible prophecy is being fulfilled and will continue to be fulfilled in the days ahead.

Chapter 16

Make God's Word Final Authority

God says in His Word that all the Scripture is inspired by Him and given to us for various reasons.

Second Timothy 3:16–17 NKJV states, "All Scripture is given by inspiration of God, and is profitable for doctrine, for reproof, for correction, for instruction in righteousness, that the man of God may be complete, throughly equipped for every good work."

God's Word will benefit us. It instructs us, corrects us, inspires us, and gives us correct doctrine or belief. It also gives us spiritual authority against the devil when we make God's Word final authority in our own personal lives. That means we have to settle in our hearts that we believe God's Word beyond what others say and beyond what circumstances may try to persuade us to believe.

We had a friend in ministry who became deceived, so we had to withdraw from him years ago. He began questioning about people in other places who had not yet heard the gospel. He felt that a good God could not send His creation to a place like hell. So he decided there was no hell except the difficult trials people face on earth. He decided that everyone was going to heaven and called the message "The Inclusion Gospel."

My late husband told him that this was nothing new, and it was "universalism." Several pastors and ministers reached out to him to try to lovingly help him see the truth, but he was convinced he was right. No one could persuade him differently.

Billy Graham, when he was younger, had a friend like this who challenged him. His friend embraced universalism. Billy said he went alone to a place to pray and told the Lord, "Lord, I may not understand everything, but I choose to make your Word final authority." Billy said he chose at that moment that he would always believe what the Bible says.

"There is salvation in no one else! God has given no other name under heaven by which we must be saved" (Acts 4:12 NLT).

Jesus said, "I am the way, the truth and the life. No one can come to the Father except through Me" (John 14: 6 NLT).

It was a turning point in Billy's life and ministry. God honored him for honoring His Word (1 Samuel 2:30). Those who believe the Bible and stay with it will see God confirm His Word with signs following (Mark 16:20).

Choose Today

If you've been wondering how to overcome temptation or how to rise above negative circumstances, Jesus is the answer. Now that you're ready to believe the Bible and receive Jesus Christ into your heart as your Lord and Savior, pray this prayer:

Lord, I surrender my life to You. Forgive me of sin. I repent and turn to You with all my heart. I turn away from everything wrong in my life. I confess You as my Lord and Savior. Cleanse me with your precious blood. I choose to believe your Word and declare what it says about me. I cast down wrong imaginations and every thought that tries to exalt itself against what the Bible says about me. I ask for your grace to help me stay committed to your Word daily. I believe You will finish the good work You have begun in me until the second coming of the Lord Jesus Christ. Thank You for your love and your strength to overcome. I declare I will overcome in this world by the blood of the Lamb and the word of my testimony (Revelation 12:11). Amen!

Write out some Scriptures that pertain to your needs and begin to speak those daily over your life. Frame the sheet of Scriptures and their references and hang it next to your bathroom mirror that you look at daily. Speak them while you are getting ready for your day. God said He will hasten to perform His Word (Jeremiah 1:12).

If you need help with locating Scriptures to speak over your life, we have a mini book, *Word Confessions for Championship Living*, by Billy Joe and Sharon Daugherty.

Confessions

The following are some of the confessions that I make from God's Word:

This is the victory that causes me to overcome in this world — my faith in Jesus and in His Word (1 John 5:4,5).

The spirit of faith is, I believe and therefore I speak (2 Corinthians 4:13).

Your Word have I hid in my heart that I might not sin against You (Psalm 119:11).

I cast down imaginations and every thought that tries to exalt itself against the knowledge of God. I bring my thoughts into captivity to the obedience of Christ and His Word (2 Corinthians 10:4–5).

No Fear

The Lord is my light and my salvation; whom shall I fear? The Lord is the strength of my life; of whom shall I be afraid? (Psalm 27:1).

God has not given me the spirit of fear; but of power, love and a sound mind (2 Timothy 1:7).

Healing

God sent His Word to heal me and deliver me from all destruction (Psalm 107:20).

Jesus said if I can believe, all things are possible; so I believe (Mark 9:23).

It is God's will that I prosper and be in health, even as my soul prospers (3 John 2).

Provision

I seek first the Kingdom of God and His righteousness, and He adds everything I need unto me (Matthew 6:33).

Children

The seed of the righteous shall be delivered (Proverbs 11:21).

The Lord will contend with him who contends with me, and He will save my children (Isaiah 49:25).

Direction

I choose to hear and follow the voice of the Good Shepherd. The stranger's voice (the devil's voice) I will not follow (John 10:4-5; 27).

I trust in the Lord with all my heart and I do not lean to my own understanding. In all my ways I acknowledge Him and He is directing my paths (Proverbs 3:5-6).

Peace

You will keep me in perfect peace, because my mind is stayed on You, Lord (Isaiah 26:3).

I let the peace of God rule in my heart and act as the umpire of my life (Colossians 3:15 AMPC).

Unsaved Loved Ones

God is not willing that _____perish, but that he/she comes to repentance (2 Peter 3:9).

It is God's will that _____be saved and come to a knowledge of truth (1 Timothy 2:4).

Whatever I bind on earth is bound in heaven and whatever I loose is loosed in heaven. I bind demon spirits from influencing_____life, and I loose _____ to receive from heaven the salvation you've provided (Matthew 18:18).

Lord, You watch over Your Word to perform it (Jeremiah 1:12).

Endnotes

Chapter 14 Examine the Evidence

[1] Sid Litke, "Is the Bible Reliable? 7 Questions," (January 2010), *www.bible.org/article/bible-reliable-sevenquestions*

[2] Ibid.

[3] "List of Prophecies Fulfilled," (March 6, 2018), Believers Portal, *www.believersportal.com/list-bible-prophecies-fulfilled*

[4] William Brown, "Stone [Mesha Stele]," (February 11, 2019), World History Encyclopedia, *www.worldhistory.org/moabite-stone-[mesha-stele]/*

[5] John D. Currid. "10 Crucial Archeological Discoveries Related to the Bible," (April 26,2018), *ESV Study Bible, Crossway, www.crossway.org/articles/tag/history/*

[6] Everette Hatcher, "The Brook Kidron and Hezekiah's Tunnel," (September 11, 2019), The Daily Hatch, *www.thedailyhatch.org*

[7] Bryant Wood, "The Walls of Jericho," (March 1,1999), Answers in Genesis, *www.answersingenesis.org*

[8] Tim Challies, "10 Most Significant Discoveries in the Field of Biblical Archeology," (April 2, 2008), *Challies, www. challies.com*

[9] Ibid.

[10] "The Tel Dan Inscription: The First Historical Evidence of King David from the Bible," (June 2022), *Biblical History Daily, www.biblicalarcheology.org*